Sammy's Walks

Dog walks in the Forest of Dean

2018

by Cheryl Mayo and Sammy

With many thanks to our fellow walkers, Rob and Jim, for their willingness to get lost in the woods.

About the authors

Cheryl came to live in the Forest with her husband in 2008, and enjoyed getting lost while learning her way around the woods after the arrival of Sammy in early 2009. She is involved in many aspects of Forest life. A particular highlight was her and Sammy's commitment to the 2010/2011 campaign HOOF, which successfully thwarted the government's attempt to sell off England's public forests. Inspired by this experience, Cheryl wrote a fantasy trilogy, *The Danae of the Forest*, under her author name CR Burman, which is enjoyed by readers from ages 8 to 80 (go to crburman.com for details).

Sammy is a committed walker and has dedicated many hours to this book, although not enough in his view. The Forest deer know him well and take little notice of his sporadic runs towards them. He is, sensibly, more wary of the boar and has given up on squirrels because they cheat and climb trees.

© Cheryl R Mayo 2018.

Contains Ordnance Survey data
© Crown copyright and database right [2018]

Published by Holborn House Ltd April 2018.

Oakdean, High Street, Blakeney, GL15 4DY

Introduction

This is the fifth edition of Sammy's Walks, thanks to the locals and visitors alike who buy it and love it. It's aimed at dog walkers, but of course you don't need a dog to enjoy walking in our Forest of Dean. Whether you're a visitor or new to the area, this book aims to help you enjoy your walks while learning your way around the Forest. To give you some context about where you are walking, I have included little bites of history in places. But if you want to know more about the long and fascinating story of the Forest of Dean, look out for Christine Martyn's highly readable book, *The Forest Revisited; a Modern History*.

The walks described here are tried and tested and mainly keep to forestry tracks and waymarked paths. In describing the walks I have tried to be consistent in terminology: a track is a hard surfaced Forestry Commission track; a trail is wide and generally well surfaced but not normally suitable for vehicles; and a path is either narrow or rough surfaced, suitable only for walkers. All stiles have dog openings or fences which can be squeezed through, or even walked around if necessary.

Before you start out, please read through the points about walking in the Forest of Dean overleaf.

If you have any comments or if you see something of interest to other dog walkers you can email us at sammyswalks@outlook.com.

Sammy and I hope our book gives you hours of walking pleasure and we look forward to seeing you in the woods from time to time, as we often do.

Cheryl

Sammy

Walking in the Forest

- The Dean is a working forest. So expect to find heavy machinery sometimes working nearby. Logging can also affect some routes, making them very rutted and muddy for a time. Very occasionally it's best to look for an alternative path or even retrace your steps and try another walk.
- Fences, stiles, signs, waymark posts and even bridges are sometimes replaced, repaired or taken out. So if you come to a point where it says there's a waymark post and there isn't, don't worry - as long as everything else looks right.
- The Sculpture Trail Trust has commissioned several more sculptures over the next three years, so if you come across one not mentioned in this book, it's because it's very new.
- There are limited facilities: Beechenhurst and the Cycle Centre both have cafes and toilets, and there are toilets at Mallards Pike and (in summer only) at Wenchford. Hopewell Colliery, which is just up the road towards Coleford from Cannop Ponds, has a cafe and a small playground - and you can also do underground tours there.
- Beechenhurst, Mallards Pike and Wenchford (in summer only) have pay and display parking. If you live in the Forest it is worth buying a Discovery Pass which gives you free parking at any of the local Forestry Commission sites where there is normally a charge (go to *http://www.forestry.gov.uk/forestry/INFD-7W5Kq6*).
- When walking on the cycle trail be aware of cyclists and keep your dog under control.
- You will occasionally come across boar: mostly they'll move off the path, but put your dog on the lead and either wait for them to go or find another path.
- There are dog litter bins at most of the starting points. However, if you are in the middle of the Forest it is quite okay to use a stick to flick the mess off the path into the undergrowth. It is definitely not okay to leave plastic bags of dog mess lying around.
- Finally, the Forest can get very muddy in wet weather even on the main tracks, so always wear suitable footwear.

Summary

Start point		Walk	Length Km	Total uphill walking (metres)	Est time	Page
Wenchford		1	2.2	58	35 min	10
		2	4.3	92	1 ¼ hrs	12
		3	5	116	1 ¼ hrs	14
	with option	3a	6.8	134	1 ½ hrs	
Mallards Pike		4	4.8	65	1 hr	20
		5	6.0	138	1 ½ hrs	22
	with option	5a	8.2	180	2 hrs	
Linear Park		6	4.0	71	1 hr	27
Cannop Ponds		7	4.7	150	1 ¼ hrs	31
		8	5.9	127	1 ½ hrs	34
Speech House: Arboretum		9	3.3	46	45 mins	40
	with option	9a	4.9	80	1 hr	
Speech House: Woodlands		10	5.0	80	1 ¼ hrs	43
		11	4.9	106	1 ¼ hrs	46
Soudley Ponds		12	3.8	114	1 hr	52
	with option	12a	5.8	191	1 ½ hrs	
Yorkley		13	4.1	100	1 hr	54
	with option	13a	5.7	147	1 ½ hrs	
Beechenhurst		14	3.8	83	55 min	58
	with option	14a	7.2	138	1hr 40min	
LongWalks	Beechenhurst	15	12.6	274	3 ¼ hrs	63
	Mallards Pike	16	13.5	235	3 ¼ hrs	68
Short Walks						73

Walk start points

Walks from Wenchford

Wenchford is a popular local picnic site. The toilet block is open during the summer months and on some weekends they open the container cafe. Blackpool Brook runs through here and is shallow enough for small children to paddle happily. However, for much of the year and during the week it is primarily the preserve of dog walkers. Logging in 2017 has heavily affected all walks so expect mud and ruts for a while.

In addition to the walks described here, you can

» take the green waymarked Blackpool Brook trail, which loops along beside the brook and into the woods nearby, for just under 1 km;
» stroll along the Brook, heading upstream along the picnic area, turning around at some point to retrace your steps;
» take the link path to Mallards Pike, which is marked by white arrows. The return distance is 5 km, mostly along good forestry tracks. You do need to cross a road which has a blind corner, so remember the dog lead.

Location: From the A48 at Blakeney take the B4431 Parkend road. Two kilometres along this road you will find the site signposted on the right. The barrier is open and closed daily, with closing times varying depending on the time of year, so take note of the specific time as you drive in. OS Grid ref: SO 654081

There is pay and display parking during the summer months.

Wenchford

Walk 1 Start point: Wenchford carpark
Length 2.2 km, total uphill walking 58 metres, est time 35 mins

This undulating walk takes you along pretty paths, crossing streams and rivulets. It follows the Mallards Pike link for a while, and then returns via a forestry track.

With the toilet block on your right and the picnic area on your left, take the track straight ahead. At the end of the parking area, take the path ahead, past a large stone and go along it to reach a second parking area. A path down to Blackpool Brook goes off to your left, but ignore this and instead follow the sign to Mallards Pike, marked by a white arrow. The path goes down, crosses a small stream and then goes back up to a T-junction. Again fol-

10

low the Mallards Pike link sign, turning left and walking along a wide path with the old railway embankment high on your left.

Shortly after another link sign, the path forks (A). The link walk continues straight ahead, but instead of following this, take the right hand path up the slope to another fork. Again take the right hand path. The path crests the hill and then goes fairly steeply down to the brook (B). Cross the brook and veer right to an intersection of paths. Take the second path in from the right *(You can also take the first path on the right, if you wish to avoid a short climb. It will take you on a pretty path straight back to the picnic site.)* After a bit the path goes quite steeply uphill for a short distance before levelling out. Continue on to a forestry track (C). Turn right and follow the track gently downhill to a point where it bends to the left and descends sharply. Instead of continuing on down, look for a path to the right (D). Take the path and follow it as it bears right, back to the carpark and picnic area.

Walk 2 Start point: Wenchford carpark
Length 4.3 km, total uphill walking 92 metres, est time 1¼ hr

This walk starts with a gentle but steady climb before coming out to a forestry track which winds its way back down again in a wide loop.

With the toilet block on your left and your back to the picnic ground, look for the path up into the woods. Go up past a green waymark, and veer right to follow the path up and then around to the left to a forestry track (A). Walk up the track, going steadily uphill, to a junction of track and paths (B).

The main track continues around to the right, but ignore this and go straight ahead, continuing uphill. The path is crossed by a small rivulet which makes it boggy at times, so you need to pick your best path through here. Continue on towards a large pylon which you can see ahead of you. Continue straight on with the pylon on your left, over another rather muddy patch, up a short slope and across a grassy area to a forestry track (C). Blakeney Hill Lodge is just to the left and directly ahead of you is a horse paddock which in spring is a mass of daffodils.

Turn right and walk along the track, passing a large enclosure on the left. Follow the track as it eventually bends around to the right and goes downhill. Keep on, passing a number of paths on both sides. After a while the track curves again to the right. There is also a path going straight ahead, but keep to the main track, passing a fenced-off disused quarry on your left, and continue steadily on down, passing under various sets of pylon and telegraph wires. The track then veers to the left and goes downhill, reaching the junction at point B.

Continue straight ahead onto a path, crossing a small stream. (*You can instead turn left and retrace your steps back to point A and the carpark at this point.*) Continue on this path, which goes down steeply to meet a junction of paths (E). Turn left and follow this path - taking the left hand fork where it divides - to arrive back at the picnic area and carpark.

Wenchford

Walks 3 and 3a Start point: Wenchford carpark
3: Length 5 km, total uphill walking 116 metres, est time 1¼ hours
3a: Join at Walk 2, point C, length 6.8km, est time 1 ½ hrs

This walk involves some steady uphill work, but in the late spring you are rewarded with a walk through some of the most beautiful bluebell woods in the Forest. You also walk along a ridge line where you catch glimpses between the trees of wide views across the Severn. The longer option of the walk is a gentle downhill stroll on a good forestry track.

14

Wenchford

With the toilet block on your right and the picnic area on your left, take the track to the end of the carpark. Ignore the path straight ahead and look for a narrow uphill path on your right, going up here to a T-junction. Turn left and continue on this path with the picnic area and Blackpool Brook below you on the left. Pass a path which goes left down to another parking area. Continue on, bending around to the right and with the brook below you in the gully on your left. Another path joins from the left. Keep straight on to a junction of paths (A).

Turn left down the hill and cross the brook. The path climbs steeply for a while and then levels out briefly before descending to a T-junction. Turn right, and follow the path gently uphill. In late spring these woods are carpeted with bluebells and are quite popular with visitors and locals alike. The path takes you to a dirt road, with a 15 mph sign just to the left (B).

Cross the road (take care: vehicles are rare but tend to move quite quickly) and continue uphill along the wide path directly ahead. The bluebells flourish here as well. The path climbs steadily up and ends at a T-junction with a track (C).

Bluebells above Wenchford

Wenchford

Turn left and follow the track. *(You can shorten the walk here by turning right and continuing on the track, passing through a barrier and then following the telegraph poles to Blakeney Hill Lodge, point E. From here, you can either continue the main walk or take the option as described below.)* Continue on to eventually reach a metalled road (D). Turn right, then take the middle road up the hill, past a white house on your right (called White House), enjoying the mass of daffodils on the verge throughout the spring. Just past the house you will see a wooden sign for Twilbee.

Keep the sign to your left and walk along the track (the metalled road ends here). You soon come to stables and the house Twilbee, set in charming grounds. (Look for the life size Red Indian and his wigwam just where the post and wire fence starts.) Continue on and just at the point where the garden meets the horse paddock you come to a telegraph pole. Halfway between this and the next telegraph pole there is a path off to the left. Take this to join another path. Turn right and keep on, with occasional glimpses of the Severn to the left, until the path ends at a track with houses ahead of you. Turn left, going past Bradley Hill Farmhouse, and continue down. Along this stretch you can catch more glimpses between the trees of the countryside across to and beyond the River Severn. At the bottom of the hill, go past a driveway and a gate with a sign Woodside House on your right and keep on, now joining a line of telegraph poles. Go past Hepworth Cottage to a junction, where a dirt road comes in from your right. Follow the line of the telegraph poles along the main track and shortly come to Blakeney Hill Lodge (E).

Option 3a: for a longer walk which takes you gently downhill on a forestry track, continue on past Blakeney Hill Lodge, joining at Walk 2, point C and following the instructions back to Wenchford.

Main walk continued

To continue this walk, leave the track just before you reach the Lodge and take the path which goes off at an angle on your right, next to the telegraph poles. It goes through large boulders (which may be hidden in the ferns in summer) and on to a pylon. Just as you reach the pylon, there is a path curving down to the right. Take this (it is quite boggy in places) to arrive at a forestry track which comes in from the left and then bends to go on directly ahead of you (F). Take the track straight ahead, continuing downhill to a point where the track bends to the left and descends sharply. Instead of continuing on down, look for a path to the right (G). Take the path and follow it as it bears right, back to the carpark and picnic area.

Walks from Mallards Pike

Mallards Pike is a popular Forest beauty spot. The lake was built by the Forestry Commission as a tourist attraction and is named after a Mr Maller, a toll-keeper who lived in a cottage near what is now the entrance to the site. Today visitors can simply sit by the lake and enjoy watching the ducks, or take to the high ropes on the Go-Ape course. Or use it as a very popular dog walk starting point. There are toilets open all year round and a burger van during summer weekends and holidays. There are plans for a cafe to open at some stage. Parking is pay and display. In addition to the walks described here you can

- » stroll around the lake edge;
- » follow the 6 km circular Adidas Running Trail;
- » take the link path to Wenchford, marked by white arrows. The return distance is 5 km.

Location: From the A48 at Blakeney take the B4431 Parkend road. Five kilometres along this road you will find the site signposted on the right. The barrier is open and closed daily, with closing times varying depending on the time of year, so take note of the specific time as you drive in. OS Grid ref: SO 637093

Mallards Pike

Walk 4 Start point: Mallards Pike carpark
Length 4.8 km, total uphill walking 65 metres, est time 1hr

This is what I describe as a "flat walk" insofar as anywhere in the Forest can be described as flat. It is gentle, with varied scenery and using good trails or paths.

Keeping the Go Ape office on your left, walk to the beginning of the Running Trail and continue until the track divides into three (A). Take the first left (marked as the cycle trail) and follow the trail as it bends around to the right and then straight on to a signposted intersection. Turn left and then immediately right, so that you are now on the rough track parallel with the cycle trail.

Continue along the track until you come to a path on your left which slopes gently upwards (B). Walk up the hill and, shortly after passing an enclosure on the left, look out for a grassy path off to the right (C). Take this path through pine trees until you come out onto a forestry track. Turn right to shortly arrive at a fork in the track, with a sign to the left saying Trafalgar Avenue (D). Take the right hand track, down a short and steep hill. At the bottom take the track to your right. It soon begins to parallel the cycle trail. Keep on until you are back at the signposted intersection. Turn left, cross over the cycle trail, and at the next junction turn right. You are now back on the running trail, from where you can follow the signs to take you back to Mallards Pike Lake.

Walks 5 and 5a Start point: Mallards Pike carpark
5: Length 6.0 km, total uphill walking 138 metres, est time 1½ hrs
5a: Length 8.2 km, total uphill walking 180 metres, est time 2 hrs

This walk takes you up to the ridge above Mallards Pike, the longish climb being rewarded with far reaching views over the Forest, for now. A steep grassy track brings you down from the ridge and from there it is an easy stroll back to the start point. The longer option follows good tracks as it winds its way gently downhill back to Mallards Pike.

Walk down to the lake edge and follow the path to your left up to the boat ramp. Turn right to cross over the lake and then turn left, following the line of telegraph poles (A).

Continue along the track for about 2 kms to a T-junction. Along the way, scan the scrubby area to the left for a sight of deer or foxes. Turn right and go up the hill to a metal gate and stile (B). *Note: you can instead turn left at the T-junction and then left again to join the Running Trail, from where it is 3 kms back to Mallards Pike.* Cross the stile and then carry on straight over the intersection, continuing uphill on a wide track.

The track levels out at a point where a considerable amount of clear felling took place a couple of years ago. The conifers are growing quickly, but you still get some far flung views across the Forest, especially beautiful in the autumn. Just past this clear felled area you come to Staple Edge Bungalows on your left, built in 1809 and once the home of Forest managers (C).

Decision point

To stay on the main walk, turn right at a waymark post opposite the corner of the stone wall around the Bungalows. This grassy path disappears downhill quite steeply to a foresty track, opposite another waymark post. Turn left and follow the track gently downhill until you come to a wide fork, which is point F on this route. Take the right hand track downhill and follow the main walk instructions from point F below.

Option 5a

For the longer option, pass Staple Edge Bungalows and keep to the main track, going gently downhill. The track reaches an intersection where there has been even more felling. Bear right, continuing downhill and past a wooden gate (D). To the left is a small, fenced pond with a rough path going past it. Ignore the path and stay on the main track. At a point where the track goes steeply downhill and bends to the left, turn sharp right (E) and continue on this new track, which winds its way around the hill.

They've done some thinning of the conifers to the left of this track so you can glimpse some good views here as well. Keep on the main track for some distance, passing various paths, until the track bends to the right, with another track coming in from the left (F). Turn left onto this track and then continue with the main walk instructions below.

Main walk continued

From point F, continue on down and just as the track levels out you'll see a waymark post with a white arrow pointing straight ahead, at the top of a path descending on your right. Take the path which goes down very steeply (and sometimes a bit slippery) to the lake, coming out at the dog dip.

Turn left and follow the path back to the carpark.

A Walk from Linear Park

Linear Park is a conservation area at the edge of the Forest town of Cinderford and as such is very popular with local dog walkers. The lakes you will pass were created in 1990 and quickly attracted a variety of wildlife. There are no facilities.

Location: The entrance to Linear Park is located on a bend on the left, just off the B4226 (Speech House Road) immediately before entering Cinderford from the direction of the Speech House. The entrance is marked by an old railway bulk container at the former Ruspidge Halt station. OS Grid reference SO6412.

Walk 6 Start point: Linear Park, Cinderford
Length 4 kms, total uphill walking 71 metres, est time 1 hr

Linear Park

The start of this walk follows the line of the old railway and at one point takes you to a map and information board so you can see just what a busy industrial place it once was. You will also pass the remains of a once flourishing colliery and on the way back you can wander past some pretty wildlife ponds.

From the carparking area nearest to the barrier, take the main path straight ahead, through the barrier. At the intersection, continue straight on, with views of Cinderford off to your right between

Linear Park

mature oaks. Go past a cycle trail sign opposite a rather bent-looking railway signal post on top of the old railway embankment, and keep on until you reach Bilson Halt. There is an information board here and photos of what it used to look like when the trail you are on was a working railway and much of the area was covered with working coal mines.

Not long past Bilson Halt you come to a rough road (A). Turn left (there might be the occasional car), going past a site with an old stone building and old trucks and vans. The road goes uphill and bends to the left, then straight on, past a treatment works, to a forestry barrier. Go through the barrier onto a wide forestry track and keep left at the fork to go gently uphill, passing a large pond on the left. Go straight on at the intersection where a rutted track goes steeply uphill on your left and continue to the next intersection. The cycle trail crosses the track here (B). Turn left onto the cycle trail and immediately come to the remains of Foxes Bridge Colliery. *(If you want to see more of the remains you can continue up the hill instead of turning left, and then go into the wide grassy area on your left to look about. Then return to the intersection.)*

If you're feeling fit, take the narrow steep path opposite the sign, past the fenced-in shaft, and climb the short distance to the top of the old spoil heap. From here you have a lovely view of Cinderford, or at least parts of it where the young pines haven't yet grown up to block it out. Return to the cycle trail and continue along, shortly going downhill with the path gradually bearing to the left.

Keep on the trail as it does a sharp right bend and shortly afterwards come to a cycle trail signpost (C). Take the path (indicated Cinderford Linear Park) and go downhill to a T-junction. Turn right and then almost immediately left, following the cycle trail markers, and go downhill again to meet up with the path you started on (D). Either turn right and go straight back to the carpark, or cross over and then take the second (wider) turn right to take the more rugged path which will also bring you back to the carpark. A pleasant diversion is to go left at the fork at the end of the pond, cross a bridge and follow this path past more ponds. At the end, there's a very interesting information board. You then turn right over another bridge and you are at the carpark.

Walks from Cannop Ponds

Cannop Ponds is a series of manmade lakes set in the steep sided Cannop Valley. It is a haven for birdlife and has a good population of swans and mandarin ducks. There is a picnic area and carparking, but no facilities except for a burger van on occasional summer weekends and holidays. Beechenhurst Lodge, with its cafe and toilets, is only a few minutes drive away however, as is the Cycle Centre.

In addition to the walks described here, you can take the path around the ponds. This can be narrow and rough in many places and one side runs close to the road so be aware of this if your dog has a tendency to run off.

Location: Enter from Speech House Road (B4226), and drive along the metalled road to reach the carpark and picnic area. OS Grid ref: SO610108

Walk 7 Start point: Cannop Ponds carpark
Length 4.7 km, total uphill walking 150 metres, est time 1¼ hrs

This walk starts out with a short ascent on a rather rough path, then steadily climbs on a forestry track. You then have a level walk along the top of the valley before joining the cycle trail to descend back to the start point. On the way you will see the HMS Victory memorial.

As you enter the carpark one way system, there is a narrow path which goes off to the left a short way in. Take this path and follow it across two bridges and then up and down above the stream until you reach a gate which leads onto a forestry track (A).

Turn left and gently ascend to a point where there is a yellow waymark on the left and a track going uphill to your right. Take the uphill track and continue to climb steadily to an intersection of

Cannop Ponds

tracks. Follow the yellow waymark direction straight ahead, still climbing. The track rises steeply for a short distance then starts to level out. Shortly after this the track intersects a path. Continue on the main track. The track curves to the right and on the bend there is another waymarked post. This time, ignore the yellow waymark and again continue on the main track. It curves right and then, staying on the main track at a fork where a rough path goes left, continue up to a gate and stile leading onto a road, with a school to your left (B). Just before reaching the gate take the path to the right. Keep on, paralleling the road and going gently downhill. There are great views across the Cannop Valley to your right.

You eventually come to a T-junction with a track, with a gate a little way up on your left (C). Go through the gate, immediately turn right and come back inside the fence line through another gate directly ahead of you. (If they still haven't moved the fallen tree, either climb it or detour into the carparking area and come back down again on the other side.) Keep straight on, paralleling the road. At a couple of places you pass some tree stumps which

Spillway at Cannop Wharf.

can make ideal seats if you want to rest a while. Very near the end of this section, where you can see the path disappearing to the left, you come across the HMS Victory memorial, to the left of the path, commemorating a special oak which stood here for 202 years.

Soon after the memorial, the path meets a track at a T-junction (D). Turn right and right again at the fork, following the main track downhill. Pass a sign warning cyclists of a right turn ahead and at the T-junction turn right to join the cycle trail. Continue downhill, past the Three Brothers sign. Follow the trail around to the right and then keep going all the way down, through a gate at one point and shortly after that arriving at a T-junction with a signpost at Cannop Wharf (E). Turn right and follow the cycle trail (direction Cannop Ponds, Cycle Centre) back to the picnic area and carpark.

If you want to take the path along the edge of the Ponds, you can access this via a path to the left of the Cannop Wharf sign. There are various exit points back up to the cycle trail along the way. If there are fishermen here, please keep your dog out of the water as it scares the fish away.

Cannop Ponds

Walk 8 Start point: Cannop Ponds carpark
Length 5.9 km, total uphill walking 127 metres, est time 1½ hrs

This walk starts out gently enough along the family cycle trail but then crosses the road into the Bixslade Valley to follow the old tramways route up the valley. The climb is well worth it as along the way you catch many glimpses of the Forest's mining heritage, passing quarries – many now defunct, some still in use – and old mine shafts, including a freeminer's gale which is still in operation. You then descend on a pretty waymarked path through the forest back down to Cannop Ponds.

Facing the ponds, walk left through the picnic area to the Family Cycle Trail direction Parkend/Coleford. Continue on until you reach a signposted junction and a sign for Cannop Wharf (A). *(You can instead take the little path on your right at the beginning of the cycle trail down to the ponds and walk along there to the stoneworks at the end. Don't let your dog into the water if there are fishermen though please.)* Just after the sign take the path to your right which goes past the stone works and take the left hand track up to the road. Cross the road (be careful, as this is a busy road and visibility either way is not good) and go through a barrier onto a forestry track. Go along the main track for a short distance, looking out on the left for a path which goes beside a line of telegraph poles (B). Take this path, and you are now on the old tramways route up the valley. You can see many of the stone slabs which are still intact. Cross over a forestry track and continue on the old tram route until you come out onto a track which ends at the gates to a quarry on your right (C).

Miners Memorial, Bixslade Valley

Cannop Ponds

It is worth making a short detour here, turning left along the track to visit the monument to the United Colliery Disaster of 1902. This is also the site of the still operating freeminer's coal mine (private property).

Return to the quarry gates and take the path to their left, through the large stones, following the telegraph poles. Continue steadily uphill, still on the old tramways route and still following the line of telegraph poles, passing a group of fenced disused mine shafts on your left and shortly afterwards a disused and overgrown quarry to your right. At the point where the telegraph poles follow a path to the left, ignore this and continue straight on. The path begins to level out and after a while comes into a more open space. Keep straight on with a wire fence briefly to the left, then keeping on with another wire fence to your right which fences a big quarry. You soon join a wide forestry track coming in from the left (D). There are quarry offices off to your right.

Go straight ahead, under the telegraph wires, and then turn left at the T-junction, along another wide track. Follow this to where it bends to the left and here go through the barrier to take the less well used track to the right (E). Some way in (between the bracken

Looking towards Cinderford with a glimpse of the Speech House

and the young trees in the summer) you can see way across the Forest, with Cinderford in the distance and, closer in, a glimpse of the Speech House perhaps.

Follow the track to a waymarked path off to the left (F), just before the mature trees begin. Follow this down into the trees, keeping right where the path diverges, until you come to the top of a fenced quarry. Follow the yellow arrow steeply down, with the fence on your left. At the point where the fence ends, the path bends to the right. Continue on quite steeply downhill, crossing a path and going straight on to reach a forestry track (G). Cross the track to take the yellow waymarked path, continuing downhill, keeping right where the path diverges, until you come to a waymarked post at a T junction with a grassy path. Veer right and then almost immediately left. Follow this path, still going downhill, crossing a rivulet and keeping on the grassy path until you reach a layby opposite Cannop Ponds. Carefully cross the road, walk along the dam and back to the carpark.

Walks from the Speech House

These walks are designed to be relatively gentle strolls, none of them being more than 5 km in length and involving little strenuous uphill walking. If you wish to push yourself and the dog harder, but in this same part of the Forest, then have a look at the walks from Beechenhurst and the two long walks at the end of the book. The first walk starts at the Cyril Hart Arboretum, located next to the Speech House. The Arboretum is named after a local historian and forestry expert and contains some 400 trees. Cyril Hart was also a Verderer of The Forest of Dean and the Speech House has been the traditional home of the Verderers' Court for over 300 years. Although now a hotel, the Court still meets there regularly. The Speech House is dog-friendly and a post walk visit to the Orangery for tea and cakes or a light lunch is well worthwhile.

The next two walks start at the the Speech House Woodlands carpark, just across the road from the Arboretum. There is a signed path from this carpark to Beechenhurst Lodge, a short distance away. Beechenhurst Lodge has toilets and a cafe, open all year round.

Location: The Arboretum carpark is on the B4226, just 200 metres along from the Speech House heading towards Cinderford. OS Grid ref: SO624118. The Speech House Woodlands carpark is a few metres further on, on your left. OS Grid ref: SO624125.

Spruce Ride in winter

Monday

Speech House

Walks 9 and 9a Start point: Cyril Hart Arboretum carpark
9: *Length 3.3 km, total uphill walking 46 metres, est time 45 mins*
9a: *Length 4.9 km, total uphill walking 80 metres, est time 1 hr*

This walk mostly follows forestry tracks and is very gentle. The last section is along Spruce Ride, an avenue of mature cherry trees which provide a spectacular pink display in the spring. You also take in Speech House Lake, surrounded by mature trees which provide their own spectacular display in the autumn.

From the carpark, go through the gate into the Arboretum and head straight across to the opposite gate. Go down the path and straight across the next intersection. There is a cleared area of forest to your left. Carry on to the next intersection and again cross straight over. The following intersection has a large oak in the middle of it (A).

Decision point

To continue the main walk, turn right and follow the track down to a junction where another track comes in sharply from the left. Continue on, passing a path coming in from the left (at two points) and then reaching an intersection with a wide track, at the brow of a hill (D). This is Spruce Ride. Turn right and follow the instructions for the main walk from point D back to the carpark.

Option 9a

To take the option, go straight over at the intersection with the oak. Carry on to a wide area with two paths coming in from the left (one is very narrow and overgrown) and the path you are on curving around to the right (B). Take the first path left (i.e. the wider one) which goes gently uphill to an intersection with an enclosure on your left. Turn right, following the main path. Pass between two large stones and at the fork go right. As the path levels out the cycle trail comes in from your left (C), marked by a cycle trail post. Just to the right is a short 'Bikes 'n' Berms' trail, opposite a timber yard on the left.

Continue on the cycle trail, going steadily downhill, passing a path on your right with a double wooden fence and then another one on your left as the trail bends to the right. After a while the trail is fenced on either side. Continue on to an intersection with a track,

Spruce Ride in spring

Speech House Lake

and warning posts for cyclists. Here leave the cycle trail and turn right and then shortly afterwards come to an intersection with three paths, almost parallel with each other, ahead of you. Take the middle path, going through an area where the track is divided by a small island of conifers bordered with logs.

The divided track comes together again just as you reach a T-junction with a forestry track. This is Spruce Ride. Turn right, and rejoin the main walk at the nearby intersection (D).

Main walk continued

From D, continue all the way down the long straight avenue of Spruce Ride to a gate at the end. About halfway, at the bottom of the dip, you pass Speech House Lake on the left.

Go through the gate into a parking area and then look to your right for the gate into the Arboretum. Go through and take any path, meandering through the trees with Speech House Field on your left, and back to the carpark.

Walk 10 Start point: Speech House Woodlands car park carpark
10: Length 5 km, Total uphill walking 80 metres, Estimated time 1¼ hrs

This is a straightforward walk which is mostly on forestry tracks, so good to do if the weather has been very wet. It includes three of the sculptures in the Sculpture Trail, but if you wish to see more of those, follow Walk 11, or buy the Sculpture Trail map and do the whole of the trail (see walks from Beechenhurst).

With Speech House Road on your right, walk along the path to the yellow waymarked post and then take the right hand path to go towards the stained glass 'Cathedral' sculpture. (You are walking along the 'nave'.) Just before the sculpture, turn left and follow the

Speech House

path to the track by Kensley Lodge. Turn left on the track, passing a gate on your right (this leads to Woorgreen nature reserve, very lovely and very muddy when the least bit wet), to go downhill and through a gate (A). Take the right hand track and follow this past a pond and a yellow waymark on the right. Keep on, passing another waymark on your left, until the track bends around to the right. There is a Gloucestershire Way marker indicating a path directly ahead, but ignore this and keep on the main track which soon starts to bend to the left (B).

On the bend there is a path going off to the left. Follow this across the open heathland, watching out for deer which can frequently be seen here, and coming out at a tarmac road (C) where you turn left.

Follow the tarmac road down quite steeply to a forestry track which goes off to the left, just before a rock set at the side of the road (D).

Take this left track, passing a Gloucestershire Way marker on the left immediately before a fork. Take the left fork, ie straight ahead and continue for some time on this relatively flat track. Initially it takes you through mixed woodland, mostly beech with a scattering of larch and oak, so particularly lovely in autumn. You then go past an enclosure on your left. After the enclosure, there are more mature trees, one of the two Coal Measure Giant sculptures, and then you come to an intersection (E) with the second of the Giant sculptures.

Turn left, up the steep hill. *Note: If you want to see the 'Hill 33' sculpture, take a short detour to the right, down the hill, but then return to point E.*

Towards the top of the hill you will pass the 'Echo' sculpture on your left, worth a detour to inspect closely. Continue up to the gate at A.

Just before this gate there is a path off to the right, marked the Gloucestershire Way. Take this path back to the carpark, but if it looks very muddy, the drier alternative is to simply keep straight on, retracing your steps and following the Sculpture Trail waymarks back past Cathedral, then along the path, taking the left fork back to the carpark.

Walk 11 Start point Speech House Woodlands carpark
Length 4.9 kms   Uphill walking 106 metres   Est time 1½ hrs

I designed this leisurely ramble after taking my daughter and some of her friends - down from London for some dog walking and autumn colour - on a walk with the aim of taking in as many of the Sculpture Trail works as we could manage in an hour or so. It's a very pleasant walk, not far, but with many stops, and mainly on forestry tracks. It also provides the option of stopping at the dog friendly Speech House for coffee or lunch. Visit www.forestofdean-sculpture.org.uk/sculptures for full descriptions of the various sculptures mentioned.

With Speech House Road on your right, walk along the path to the yellow waymarked post and then take the right hand path, going towards the stained glass 'Cathedral' sculpture, which depicts many scenes of Forest life (it was done before the wild boar arrived, so you will search in vain for those). Just before the sculpture take the left path and follow the path to the track by the house, Kensley Lodge (one of the old Forestry Commission lodges). Turn left, passing a gate on your right (the gate leads to Woorgreen Nature Reserve, about 200 metres in and to the left - muddy when wet), to go downhill to the gates (A).

Go through and then keep straight on, downhill, soon coming to the clever and beautiful 'Echo' sculpture on your right, which is a replica of the hillside behind it (not a cast mirror image). Continue downhill to an intersection with one of the two Coal Measure Giant sculptures to the left (the other is 300m along the track to the right). Cross straight over and, just after passing a forestry track to the right, you will come across 'Hill 33', which is rapidly returning to the Forest. Just past 'Hill 33' take the path to the right, going downhill to join a forestry track (B). Turn right, and immediately cross a wide outfall, looking to your right across the water to find the 'Cone and Vessel' sculpture, a large pine cone and acorn.

Keep on this track, crossing a stream and then come to a Sculpture Trail marker on your right, with a path opposite, going left into the trees. Take the path to a bench, and, sitting on the bench, look up to your left to the sign on the tree saying 'Silenzio'. Enjoy the quiet and then return to the track, turning left to keep going in the same direction you were headed before you made the detour. You soon come to another Sculpture Trail marker on your right, opposite a path to the left. Stand at the entrance to the path and look to your right, by the tree with the very knobbly trunk, to a circle of earth and a stone marker with an inscription saying 'Clear Circle, Define Border'. Now go down this path, cross the little stream (which may be dry in the summer), go between the bamboo clumps and follow the path as it goes up and to the left, until you come to a gate (C). Go through the gate, and you are now on the cycle trail

Speech House

(once a railway line). Turn left, and go along the trail, watching out for cyclists. Pass a Sculpture Trail sign pointing in the opposite direction to which you are walking and keep on, admiring the beech and oak to your right. Ahead you can see a wooden barrier across the trail, but before you get there, stop where there is a Sculpture Trail marker on a fence post to the left. Peer down between the trees to find the life-sized metal deer sculpture.

Now keep on to the wooden barriers, going through where it says No Cycles, to come to the 'Iron Road' with its beautiful Forest (and other) symbols - both natural and man-made - carved into the old sleepers. Go through the next barrier to reach White Gates (D). You will return to the gates, but first of all take a detour down the right hand path (not the main track, but the path indicated by the Sculpture Trail marker), going downhill a short distance to see 'Black Dome', a mound of black charcoal? earth? with short pieces of protruding logs. Follow the marker where the path curves to the right towards a bench. Down on the left, by the man-made canal, is the sculpture 'Fire and Water Boats', a group of canoes sitting there in the shallow waters. Now follow the next marker to take the path uphill, going past one of nature's own sculptures - the trunk of a wonderful ancient beech tree whose top half, sheared off in some storm, lies in the dip behind. The path brings you out to the cycle trail, where you turn right to come back to the white gates (D).

Go through the gates and take the right hand track, then right again at the next fork. (Note the white Yaşasin sculpture through the trees to the left.) Go up the hill, and about halfway up, follow a path which goes left into the trees. Here, on the hill to your left, you will find 'Dead Wood', a series of grave like stone slabs set in the forest floor. Return to the main track and continue up the hill past the Sculpture Trail signs, to reach an intersection of tracks (E).

To stay on the walk route, turn left, up the hill. Or you can make a short detour, turning right, then taking the first path left, to see the 'Heart of Stone' sculpture. If you do that, return to point E and continue up the short steep hill towards the open gravelled area where 'Place' - the sculpture of what looked like a giant chair - used to be. As of March 2018 they are building something new

Speech House

there. With your back to the sculpture and the views, take the left path at the fork. Follow this winding path, beautiful in autumn with its oak and beech, as it skirts above and around Beechenhurst, all the way to a gate.

If your dog has a tendency to run off and explore, put him on the lead now as for the rest of the walk you will parallel a very busy road, although you will hardly be aware of this. Go through the gate following the Speech House link sign and keep on the path, shortly seeing the Speech House appearing through the trees above you to the right. At a point where there is another Speech House link sign at the bottom of a grassy path leading up to the Hotel (F), go through the gate on your left, and a little way in you will come to a stand of yew trees, with a marker explaining their historical significance. Go back to the gate and turn left, continuing on until you reach the carpark.

A Walk from Soudley Ponds

Soudley Ponds is a series of man-made ponds set in a small steep-sided valley and surrounded by huge Douglas fir trees. The path around the ponds provides a beautiful and easy stroll for local people, visitors and dog walkers. There are no facilities, but the Dean Heritage Museum which is located on the opposite side of the road at the far end of the Ponds, has a cafe and dogs are welcome.

Location: The carpark is located on the minor Soudley to Littledean Road, about a kilometre along on the right hand side (there is a sign as you turn into the parking area). OS Grid ref: SO668114

Soudley Ponds

Walks 12 and 12a Start point: carpark on the Soudley-Littledean Rd
12: Length 3.8 km, total uphill walking 114 metres, est time 1 hr
12a: Length 5.8 km, total uphill walking 191 metres, est time 1½ hrs

This walk starts out with a fairly stiff climb, rewarded by the views across the Severn from the Blaize Bailey viewpoint. After that, it's all downhill, along a path which follows the contour of the hill – with some great forest views along the way–and then meets up with the longer option to descend to the carpark. The option undulates but gradually takes you back down via a large loop. There are lovely views across the valley in the latter part of the walk.

Walk through the barrier at the back of the carpark to a meeting of three forestry tracks. Take the middle track and climb steadily up to the top. Shortly after the track bends to the right, you come to an intersection of tracks with a house on the left. Go straight on and continue up for a little way to a fork in the tracks and a yellow waymark pointing left (A). Follow the waymark and you shortly come to the Blaize Bailey viewpoint, giving you panaromic views across the Severn and up to the Cotswolds. Retrace your steps to the fork.

The view from Blaize Bailey, Soudley Ponds

52

Soudley Ponds

Decision point

To continue the main walk, go back down to the track opposite the house. Turn left to follow the path gently downhill. It's peaceful and pretty along here and in winter you might get views between the trees to the right. You eventually come out at a forestry track (C). Opposite you is a grove of beech trees which are splendid in the autumn. Turn right on this track with the beech trees on your left, and wind your way downhill until you are back at the carpark.

Option 12a

For the option, take the right hand track (as you face the waymarked post with the lookout on your left). From this point you simply continue on the main track, passing a number of paths on both sides. At one point another track comes in from the left (B) and after a while the track sweeps downhill around to the right, giving you lovely views over the valley with some houses down below. There is a brief uphill shortly after this, going up to a grove of beech trees on the left. Here the track joins the path (on your right) from the main walk (C). Continue on the main track which bends around to the right and then winds its way downhill back to the carpark.

A Walk from Yorkley

There are numerous laybys beside most Forest roads where locals park to start their dog walks. I have chosen this one just outside the village of Yorkley as a good example of a "local walk".

> **Walks 13 and 13a Start point: Layby outside Yorkley, on the right just past the delimited speed signs heading towards Parkend.**
> *13: Length 3.7 km, total uphill walking 87 metres, est time 1 hr*
> *13a: Length 5.7 km, total uphill walking 147 metres, est time 1½ hrs*

This walk starts out on a forestry track, and then takes you further up into the woods to go past Danby Lodge, formerly a forest manager's lodge and now a private home. Enjoy lovely views across the valley before descending via a grassy track back to your start point. The longer option misses Danby Lodge, but I have noted where you can make a short detour to see it if you wish.

Go through the barrier and along the track, with young beech and oak and conifers either side. Pass under the telegraph wires and continue straight across the intersection with a path (A). Continue on the main track which soon bends around to the right. At this point the valley falls away quite steeply to your left. Go past an uphill path on your right and descend steadily for some way. Pass under more telegraph wires. Follow the main track until it climbs uphill and sweeps around to the right. As you reach the crest you will see that the track descends and curves right.

Decision point

To stay on the main walk, look out here for a wide path which goes up on your right (B). If it's muddy at the bottom, use the narrow path to the left which you can see joins the wide one a few metres ahead.

Follow the path up and around to the right. A little way along there is a bench set at a point to take advantage of a spectacular view through the trees. The path climbs steadily to a fork. Keep left, passing Danby Lodge above you on your right and admiring the views to your left at a point where a path comes in to join yours. At the next fork go right and pass through a gate next to a barrier, then walk up to a gravel road. The Lodge gates are to your right. Take the rough forestry road which goes off to the left (NOT the path to the left of the forestry track). Pass a track on your right which leads to some houses and shortly afterwards you come to an intersection with a path (D). The lines of telegraph poles also intersect here. Turn right and follow the instructions below for the main walk from point D.

Option 13a

For the option, continue downhill on the main track, continuing to bear right. The track winds its way around the contour of the hill with paths and rutted and steep logging tracks off to either side. Ignore them and keep to the main track, which starts to ascend, at first gently and then more steeply. As the track levels out you come to a five way junction (C). Ignore the track immediately

Yorkley

to your right, which heads back in the direction you have come from, and take the right hand track which goes up the hill.

Cross an intersection with a path with a no riding symbol, continue on, ignoring another path to the right and noting the old quarry to your left. Go past a grassy path to the left to reach a line of telegraph poles. Take the path off to the right (the one with another no riding symbol) and follow the line of telegraph poles through a grassy area with the outskirts of the village of Yorkley to your left. Keep following the telegraph poles to an intersection with a dirt road, with a couple of houses on the other side of the road and off to the right (D).

Cross the road and then follow the main walk instructions below. *Note: if you wish to see Danby Lodge, turn right along the dirt road and the Lodge is a short distance along, directly ahead.*

Main walk continued

From point D, go downhill on the path below the telegraph poles, admiring the views straight ahead. Cross an intersection with a narrow path, and continue down to the track at point A. Turn left and retrace your steps to the layby.

A Walk from Beechenhurst

In the summer months Beechenhurst Lodge and picnic site attracts thousands of visitors every weekend and throughout the holidays. There is a cafe and toilets, barbecue facilities, a climbing wall and children's playground. There is also a Junior Go Ape ropes course. However, you don't need to go very far from the main site to get away from the crowds.

The Lodge used to be the site of Speech House Hill Colliery, a not very successful mine which was eventually acquired by the Crawshay family and used for ventilation and emergency exit purposes from other mines they owned nearby. The site was closed about 1945 and eventually transformed into the current Lodge and picnic area. In recent years the smooth grassy picnic grounds proved most attractive to boar, to such an extent that a (low key) boar proof fence has now been built around the whole area.

In addition to the walk described here you can follow the 4.5 miles long Sculpture Trail, which starts at Beechenhurst. (Visit www.forestofdean-sculpture.org.uk/sculptures for full descriptions of the various sculptures mentioned.)

You can also just do Option 14a, making the Speculation car park and picnic area your start point. And there is a 12.6 km walk from Beechenhurst included in the long walks section of this book.

Location: Beechenhurst is located between the Speech House and Coleford on the B4226. From the Speech House, head towards Coleford, going down the steep winding road. The turnoff to Beechenhurst is on your right and well marked. Parking is pay and display. The barrier is open and closed daily, with closing times varying depending on the time of year, so take note of the specific time as you drive in. OS Grid ref: SO614120

Speculation is located just off the B4234. Continue past Beechenhurst towards Coleford, turning right at the next intersection. Go past the Cycle Centre and Speculation is clearly marked not far beyond it on your right.

Beechenhurst

Walks 14, 14a Start point: Beechenhurst Lodge.
14: Length 3.8 km, total uphill walking 83 metres, est time 55 min
14a: Length 7.2 km, total uphill walking 138 metres, est time 1hr 40 min

This relatively gentle walk combines good tracks with forest paths. It takes you to Speculation, the site of a coal mine which opened in 1800 and remained in production until 1925. The longer option takes in more industrial history, going past the Mierystock bridge and tunnel before leading you deeper into the Forest to walk around a delightful and peaceful fishing pond, which were once the Waterloo Colliery screens.

Beechenhurst

Starting at the Junior GoApe course, go through the boar proof gate and continue up the slope to an intersection.

Turn left, going downhill to a Sculpture Trail marker (A). To see 'The Heart of Stone' sculpture follow the marker down the path a little way and off to the left, then come back up to the main track at point A. Turn left to continue downhill on this track. Pass two Sculpture Trail markers pointing ahead. Ignore the third marker, keeping left (or follow it up briefly to see the sculpture Yaşasin, then return). Take the path down to the White Gates (B).

Go through the gate. Just to your left you will see another Sculpture Trail marker. Follow this to see the 'Black Dome' sculpture and, a little further along, the 'Fire and Water Boats' which are below the path at the side of the old industrial waterway. Keep following the markers back to the track at a point with another marker pointing right. The White Gates are off to your right, but turn left to the T-junction (C) with a cycle trail marker ahead of you.

Turn left and after about 60 metres look out for a narrow path

Mierystock Tunnel

Beechenhurst

on the right. Follow this (the path can be damp underfoot in wet weather) to a fork. The path straight ahead goes to a dirt road, but keep right and come out on to a wide undulating grassy area. You will see the dirt road and parking area off to the left. You are now on the site of the former Speculation Colliery.

Follow the edge of the undergrowth around to the right to a small hill with a fenced off area on the top. Go up there to see the mine shaft. It's rather overgrown and surrounded by bracken so difficult to spot in the summer. Now go across to the dirt road, turn right and start to take the right hand fork. Almost immediately there is a path on your right going gently uphill. Take this and turn right onto a wide track. You are now on the cycle trail (D).

Decision point

To stay on the main walk, turn right and follow this wide trail as it winds along the hill above a valley. It eventually makes a big right hand sweep, going downhill, and comes out at a signposted intersection with another part of the cycle trail (H). Cross over the intersection to turn right through the wooden barrier. Follow this past, or over, the beautiful 'Iron Road' sculpture. Go through another wooden barrier to come out at the White Gates (B).

Go back through the white gates and take the right hand track up to the fork.

Again take the right hand track, going back the way you came originally. But this time, take the left hand path about halfway up to visit the 'Dead Wood' sculpture amongst the larch trees on the hillside to your left. Then return to the main track, turning left up the hill to come out at an intersection. Walk down the track in front of you to pass through the boar gate to the Lodge and car park.

Option 14 a

For the longer option, turn left on the cycle trail at point D. After a short distance you come to a cycle trail signpost at a fork. Take the left fork, signposted Branch to Lydbrook. Now follow this trail for some way, looking out on your right for a fenced in mine entrance (heavily overgrown but you can spot it by the red marker on the fence post) and also a pile of red bricks – traces of the area's industrial past. Eventually you come to Mierystock Bridge (E).

The detour to the fishing ponds starts here, so if you don't wish to follow this, pick up the instructions again at point E below.

Continue on the trail, past the Mierystock Tunnel and its viewing point, and shortly come to a point where the trail bends left, with a rough path going off to the right (it's very rough and can be very muddy as well) (F). Take this right hand path and follow it to an open area. Veer a little left to cross to a forest track and turn right, following the track to where it splits and loops back on itself. On your right is a path which will bring you to the edge of the fishing pond. Once upon a time these were colliery screens, where the coal was washed and graded after being brought to the surface. This is a beautiful and tranquil spot, despite the ever present hum of traffic behind you. You can walk around the edge to take in the different perspectives and the mass of water lilies (be careful not to head off at a tangent into the woods), or you can just stop awhile and enjoy the rest.

Now retrace your steps: go back to the track, turn left and then left again to cross the open area and then take the path back to the cycle trail. Turn left and return to Mierystock Bridge (E).

Cross the bridge and continue straight on, through a wooden barrier, going gently uphill on a stony path. To your right is a spoil heap, now just part of the Forest. The path brings you out on to a wide track, which is also part of the cycle trail (G). Turn right and go gently downhill. Pass Speculation on your right and rejoin the main walk at the decision point, D.

Beechenhurst

Waterloo Colliery Screens

A Long Walk from Beechenhurst

See Walks from Beechenhurst for general information and directions.

> **Walk 15 Start point: Beechenhurst Lodge**
> *Length 12.6 km, total uphill walking 274 metres, est time 3¼ hrs*

A good three hour or so ramble through the Forest, taking in old colliery sites in various stages of disappearance, along forest paths and wider tracks, with (mostly) gentle slopes and open views over heathland and through trees. A good day's outing and the dog will love it too. You have to cross a busy road, so remember the lead.

Long Walks

Long Walks

Facing the large Beechenhurst information map, walk up the right hand main trail ahead. Go through the heavy wooden gate in the boar proof fence and continue up the winding path, past the Mycelium sculpture following the tree roots (which may or may not be working), until you reach the top. This is where 'Place' - the much loved sculpture otherwise known as the Giant's Chair - used to be. In March 2018, when we went to press, a new sculpture was going up here.

Continue on past the new sculpture to the main track, and turn left downhill. Where the track does a sweep to the right, keep left, following the Sculpture Trail marker. The track now becomes a path, and a little way ahead the 'Heart of Stone' sculpture is off to your left. Admire it, then return to the path, continuing downhill then steeply and briefly uphill to go through a gate and onto the cycle trail (B).

Note: if the weather has been very wet, the next section of the walk will be quite muddy. To avoid this, you can turn right on the cycle trail to reach White Gates, then turn left at the signpost in the direction Drybrook Road Station, then left again at the T-junction. About 60 metres along look out for a narrow path off to your right. This is point C. Take the path, following the directions from point C below.

Cross the cycle trail, go over the stile (the dog goes under the fence) and down the path with a wooden fence on the left. The path now becomes uneven and muddy in places, even in dry weather, but it takes you through a pretty valley with a stream running through it. At the end of the fence, head downhill towards the road to a footbridge. Don't cross the bridge, but turn right just before it and follow the path as it winds its way along to eventually reach another footbridge - note the old man-made drainage channels to the left. Cross this bridge and follow the path to the right, going steadily uphill and coming out at a forestry track. Turn right onto the track and go uphill to the crest, where there is a narrow path going off at a sharp angle to your left (C). If you come to the cycle trail signpost you have gone too far.

Take the narrow path, which in summer can be quite overgrown

Long Walks

and in winter can be rather puddly. Near the end, bear right at the fork to come out to a wide grassy area. This is Speculation (see Walk 14 if you wish to try and see the old mine shaft). Cross over the grass to the road and carpark and at the fork in the road, take the left track. Pass a wide but generally muddy path on the left and then take the next narrow path left up to the cycle trail. Turn left, and at the signpost take the left hand fork in the direction Branch to Lydbrook. Now follow this path for some distance to Mierystock Bridge, paralleling the line of the old railway (D). *Note: if you wish to see Waterloo Screens, follow the instructions in Walk 14a.*

Turn right over the bridge, noting the tunnel in the cutting to your left. Go through a wooden barrier and walk steadily uphill, passing an old spoil heap on the right, to an intersection with the cycle trail, and a cleared area opposite.

Take the path straight up, under the power lines. After you pass a track to the left, the path climbs steeply for a short while to a barrier. Go through the barrier onto a forestry track. Serridge Lodge, one of the old Forestry Lodges, is off to your right. Turn left, past another barrier, then continue on this track along the ridge line with lovely

Long Walks

views to the left in winter. A little way before the track bends sharply to the left, you will come to a track on your right. Take this, going past Trafalgar Lodge. Follow the track around to the left - noting the stones on your right which mark the site of the Trafalgar colliery - and go past the houses onto a narrow path. The chance of sighting deer along this path are quite high. Keep going for some way until you eventually come to a metalled track. Turn right and go a short distance to Drybrook Road Station, at an intersection with the cycle trail (E).

Turn left, in the direction Mallards Pike, and keep on the cycle trail to an intersection marked by hazard posts. *Note: if you wish to take a shortcut, continue straight ahead and follow the cycle trail markers to Dilke Bridge (point G) passing Foxes Bridge Colliery on the way.*

Turn right, uphill, and continue on this track to a metal barrier. Go through and come out at a high spot where a metalled track intersects with a number of paths. The views across the open heathland are wonderful and you may well spot deer in there also (F).

Turn left and stay on the metalled track until the tarmac ends at a point where the track bends sharply to the right with a yellow waymark pointing right. Don't follow the waymark, but turn left onto another metalled surface which soon degenerates into a rough dirt track which slopes gently upwards to a junction with another path. Continue straight on, with open cleared land to your right, and an enclosure to your left.

Pass a gate into the enclosure and then, as the track bends to the right you will see, on your left, another gate into the enclosure. Between you and the gate is a path. Cross over to the path and turn right to follow it past the end of the enclosure. Keep on, going downhill to reach another open area with views of Cinderford off to the left. Go past the end of another enclosure and keep on for a little way until you come to a fork. Take the grassy path to the left, soon going downhill, and negotiate a small muddy patch to come out on to the cycle trail. Turn right and follow the trail to Dilke Bridge (G).

Just after the bridge, turn right at the signpost to follow the direction Mallards Pike. Go past spoil heaps and Lightmoor Colliery (you may spot a peacock and/or a pig), through a gate and straight on up the hill to a T-junction. Turn right to go through the large stones and follow the track, curving to the left at the point where it becomes more of a grassy path straight ahead, and coming out at a junction of paths. Take the right hand track to an intersection with a large oak in the middle and a marker saying M3 on the right. Continue straight on. At the next intersection, again keep straight on, and again at the next intersection, which will lead you to the Arboretum. Go through the gate and straight across to the exit (H). Or you may choose to have a look around, and perhaps take advantage of the benches to have a short break.

Once you leave the Arboretum (with your dog on its lead) follow the track up to the main road, taking the left hand fork. You will see the Speech House off to your left. Cross the road into the grassy area straight ahead. Be very careful - the traffic moves fast here. There is no path, but keep the small wooden enclosure (which appears to be protecting holly and brambles) on your right, and walk straight down until you can see a path below you. Head for the path - there is the beginning of a narrow path to help you - and when you reach it, turn left and follow the Sculpture Trail markers. Pass an arrow pointing back up to the road just below Speech House - and keep on, going downhill, to go through a wooden gate. Pass a commemorative oak on your left. Immediately after the oak, ignore the marker which points right and follow the black arrow to take the narrow, and somewhat steep, downhill path. Follow this to a gate in the boar proof fence, go through the gate, and you are back at Beechenhurst, on the opposite side of the Lodge from the main carpark.

A Long Walk from Mallards Pike

See Walks from Mallards Pike for general information and directions.

Walk 16 Start point: Mallards Pike car park
Length 13.5 km, total uphill walking 235 metres, est time 3 ¼ hrs

This long walk takes in many aspects of the Forest, walking on wide tracks, narrow paths which wend through quiet woods, and parts of the cycle trail. It involves quite a lot of steady uphill work in the first half, rewarded with wide views, but also offers the opportunity to visit a beautiful lake (mud permitting). Make sure you take the dog's lead as you have to cross a busy road twice.

Long Walks

With the Go Ape office on your left, walk to the beginning of the Running Trail and continue on until the track divides into three. Take the right hand path and continue along this undulating and slightly winding track for some time until you come to a T-junction. Turn right and, passing a track off to your right, go up the hill to a metal gate and stile (the stile can be avoided by scrambling up the bank to the left of the gate) (A). Cross the stile to a junction of tracks, and turn left. Now follow this track for some distance, winding up and downhill, passing a couple of enclosures with young beech. In the summer there are foxgloves and, later, large rosebay willow herb, in amongst the beech and the occasional rowan with their rich red berries. The track slopes down and comes to a fork, where you keep left, continuing downhill. Cross a stream with a path running alongside and now go uphill. As you crest the hill you will see Cinderford ahead of you. Go down to the road, putting your dog on the lead on the way (B).

Across the road to your right is the entrance to Linear Park. But you are going to go straight across the road to a narrow path in the grass, just to the left of the telegraph pole, and hard to see from this side. Be very careful - the road is busy, traffic moves fast and there is a blind bend to the right.

Go along the narrow path towards a metal gate into a rugby field. Just before the gate, turn left to wend your way uphill through the trees, coming out onto a path which is the cycle trail. Turn right and head along the trail to where there are two cycle trail markers in quick succession - the first indicates a downhill path to the right, but keep on to the second marker where there is also a sign saying Family Cycle Trail and a white arrow pointing up the path. Turn left to follow the white arrow to reach another intersection with the cycle trail and a signpost. Turn right and follow the trail, passing the remains of Foxes Bridge Colliery, to an intersection with hazard posts (C).

Turn left here, uphill. The track levels out after a while and then takes you to a metal barrier. Go through the barrier and onto a metalled track, admiring the views across the Forest which suddenly open up in front of you.

Long Walks

Cross the metalled track to the stone marker and then take the diagonal path which is immediately to the right of the marker (not the path with yellow waymarks), crossing the heathland to arrive at a wide forestry track (D). This is another good place to spot deer, and sometimes foxes.

At this point you have a choice. If the weather has been reasonably dry and you don't mind a bit of rough, possibly muddy, walking, then follow the instructions in the next paragraph. The reward for your effort is to walk around the beautiful and mostly hidden Woorgreen Lake. Woorgreen is the result of open cast mining which took place in this very swampy area up until 1981. Rather than refill the hole, they let it fill with water and it's now a beautiful nature reserve. However, much of the path is terrible in winter and in very wet weather, slippery with clay and rutted, and is not to be recommended. So, if that's the case, turn right at point D and follow the track as it bends to the left, goes past a small pond and then to an intersection. Turn left, go through the gate ahead and continue up, walking alongside the high hedge which surrounds Kensley Lodge until you reach the gate into the Lodge, with paths off to your right. This is point E. Follow the instructions from point E below.

To walk around Woorgreen, from point D turn left and head towards the trees about 100 metres up on your right. Just past the point where the trees start, take the wide but rough path to the right (this is the worst section so if it's passable, the rest should be). Follow this alongside a little stream and ahead you will soon catch a glimpse of the lake. At a T-junction with yellow waymarks, turn right and take the grassy path which parallels the lake. Follow the path around to another yellow waymark pointing right. There is a notice here asking you not to allow your dog into the water at this point. (If you would like to give the dog a swim, carry on around the lake edge for about 50 metres to an area set aside for a dog dip. The path is often very muddy so the dog will need the swim by the time he gets there. To get back to the route, take the path away from the lake and turn right. You are then on the track leading out of Woorgreen.) To leave the lake, follow the path leading away and turn right, following this rough path back, through a gate near the high hedge surrounding Kensley Lodge. Turn left and walk alongside the hedge until you reach the gate into the Lodge, with paths off to your right (E).

From point E, follow the Sculpture Trail markers to the 'Cathedral' sculpture, then turn right along this path, taking the left fork to a carpark. Go through the carpark and down to the road, dog on the lead.

Go to about the second oak on your right along the verge and then cross very carefully to the grassy area opposite, picking your way ahead and veering right through the trees to the Arboretum carpark which you can see ahead of you. Go into the Arboretum and turn right, following the path with Speech House field on your right, to the gate at the far end. Go through the gate, turn left and go through another gate onto a wide forestry track. This is Spruce Ride (F).

Long Walks

From point F, follow the Ride straight down, crossing over the first intersection and then walking between the huge cherry trees (gorgeous in spring, full of luscious fruit for the taking in summer) to the second intersection, with Speech House Lake on your right. Turn right towards the lake but then turn immediately left, and follow this path with the lake and the fishing stands on your right and the stream on your left. Please don't let your dog into any part of the lake if there are fishermen there, as it ruins their fishing for the day.

Just where the path begins to curve to the right, following the lake, the path forks. [There were lots of marked up trees here in late summer 2017, so if there's logging going on, go back to the end of the lake and turn left up the hill to reach a forestry track. Turn left and you will come to point G, this time with the Trafalgar Ave sign on your left.] Take the left fork to stay alongside the little stream. It winds its way through the trees, crosses the stream and then goes along beside a fence to reach a forestry track. Turn right, go over the stream again and then continue up the hill ahead of you to a junction at the crest with a sign saying Trafalgar Avenue on your right (G).

Stay left and about 100 metres along, take the path which goes left through the pine trees and comes out at a grassy track. Turn left, downhill to reach a track parallel with the cycle trail. Turn right and you will soon come to a T-junction, where you do a dog leg left then right, to go onto the cycle trail at a point where there is a signpost. Follow the signpost in the direction Mallards Pike 1.5 km. The trail narrows and bends to the left and then comes out at a wide track. Turn right and follow the cycle trail signs to Mallards Pike.

Ten Short walks

The following walks don't need maps. They are short, easily accessed and on good tracks, and are listed here for those who have puppies which can't go for long walks yet, or for dog walkers with limited mobility, or if you have a stroller/toddler as well as a dog to handle. They're also great for when the dog's already had one proper walk that day and you just need to take him around the block, as it were.

Bathurst Park, Lydney
Whitecross Road, Lydney GL15 5DQ

A cafe and children's play area (no dogs) with a large open park beyond where dogs can run off lead.

Cannop Ponds
See Walk 7 for directions and detailed information

Stroll along the cycle trail as far as the stone works, and back again

Linear Park, Cinderford
See Walk 6 for directions and detailed information

Stroll along the main track for as far as you wish, and back again, or follow the path around the lakes.

Lydney Lake
Lakeside Gardens, Lydney GL15 5RH. Hidden between the rugby club and the bypass, parking on Lakeside Gardens or nearby.

Stroll around, making sure your dog doesn't disturb the fishermen.

Lydney Harbour
Harbour Road, Lydney GL15 4ER (continue on past the Station as far as you can go)

Walk around this Ancient Scheduled Monument and/or take the canal path towards Lydney and back again.

Mallards Pike
See Walk 4 for directions and detailed information.

Walk around the Lake or follow the Running Trail for a distance, and then walk back again.

Short Walks

Soudley Ponds

See Walk 12 for directions and detailed information

Walk around the ponds, crossing over either at the first bridge, or, for something longer, the second bridge. Take care not to let your dog disturb the fishermen.

Speech House Arboretum

See Walk 9 for directions and detailed information

Very popular dog walking in a large (and enclosed) space.

Spruce Ride

Signposted entrance to carpark on the road from the Speech House heading towards New Fancy and Parkend. Or walk through the Arboretum, and Spruce Ride is to the left as you go through the far gate.

This wide Ride is worth a visit in the spring when the cherry trees are in full bloom. Walk down and back up again.

Wenchford

See Walk 1 for directions and detailed information.

Walk down to and through the picnic area, up the ramp and back to the carpark; or take the track from the carpark straight along to Blackpool Bridge and then return, via the picnic area if you wish.

Printed in Great Britain
by Amazon